The Threshold of the Year

The Threshold
of the Year

Poems by Mary Kinzie

University of Missouri Press
Columbia & London, 1982

University of Missouri Press, Columbia, Missouri 65211
Library of Congress Catalog Card Number 81–16161
Printed and bound in the United States of America

Library of Congress Cataloging in Publication Data

Kinzie, Mary.
  The Threshold of the Year
  (A Breakthrough book; no. 36)
  I. Title. II. Series.
PS3561.T5915   811'.54   81–16161
ISBN 0–8262–0361–2   AACR2

Grateful acknowledgment is made to the following magazines for publishing these poems and for allowing them to be reprinted:
Bennington Review, "To Gustavus Adolphus in Basic Training," "The Third Casket," "Old People's Holiday," and "Coming On Again"; *Johns Hopkins Magazine,* "Period Pieces"; *The New Republic,* "Reading During Marriage," "Asked to Recall a Moment of Pure Happiness," and "The Quest"; *Poetry,* "Novum Organum"; *Salmagundi,* "Des Knaben Wunderhorn," "Heroic Statue in a Garden Run Wild," "Gabriel," "Claude Lorrain's 'Herdsman,' 1655," "List," "Zeitblom: His Commentary on the Pictures," "Scenes from the Liturgy," and "Negatives"; *Southern Review,* "Minor Landscape" and "Venice Rising"; *Yale Review,* "The Tattooer."

I would like to thank the MacDowell Colony in Peterborough, New Hampshire, where six of these poems were written.

for Jon Arvid

Acts of Contrition

Once the ward had answered to my key
the past swept out on sun. Iron gave way,
darkness withdrew before me, but the scene
shook at the strain, lightheaded, stiff with shade.

The Devins Award for Poetry

The Threshold of the Year is the 1982 winner of The Devins Award for Poetry, an annual award originally made possible by the generosity of Dr. and Mrs. Edward A. Devins of Kansas City, Missouri. Dr. Devins was President of the Kansas City Jewish Community Center and a patron of the Center's American Poets Series. Upon the death of Dr. Edward Devins in 1974, his son, Dr. George Devins, acted to continue the Award.

Nomination for the Award is made by the University of Missouri Press from those poetry manuscripts selected by the Press for publication in a given year.

Contents

The Threshold of the Year

Minor Landscape

Out in the north beyond that stand of trees,
new-green, with pink and chilly russet strata
much like light glowing in the cruces,
is the hiding place. Brindled cows
investigate a white-hot stack of ancient
mulch: they're peaceable, however large
their jaws upon their tiny frames. Virginals,
mild French, and laxer agricultural
recourses raise their necessary sounds,
which are hardly to be heard from far and here.

Landed gentlemen direct their stubby
shanks and modicum of lace toward
a tufted hill where, against the mossy
fall of air into a lightless valley,
their torsos seem unearthly thin and long,
their shoulders, simple blades. White clay pipes
glimmer in long arcs beside their hands
while words come batted by the past at intervals,
disjoint and plump. The queer adornments
of their tongue, its queerer strengths, are manly

stasis in the moral views, the craft
of state, the way to seed adjacent fields
obliquely as to rows, how force the plum,
how breed the spicy hound, how stave the cooling
marriage with more home delights. Their moods?—
a mystery, inconsequent, perverse.
But pain is real enough and difficult
dark passions that meet them in the curling wood
beyond the fading hill, the sun-smoked mulch,
the quiet brindled cows, and playing wives.

through filmy flood and camera eye
seems linked by accident to water,
    painted in and lapping
    at the top of the least,
last visible line of stone, old walls
against the Adriatic ridged like
crocodiles, bumpy, scaled, lazily
    alert, flush to the eyes

in drifting mud. Sacred arches turn
alluvial and sly, Egyptian,
    Moorish. Churches' brazen
    vanes, Christ's jeweled orb
burn ambergris as the Byzantine
metalled ground from which madonnas, prim,
smug, and sallow gaze indulgently
    at our pointed worship.

City of coin and marriage, full of
frescoed, flaming eyes, indentations
    in bone: here one is looked
    steadily upon as
expected object, giving homage,
pinned to latent visibilities
by their syncretic god, part windy
    summer gust, part rotten

prow, part pander in the square and sheikh
apprised of loop and link in woven
    braid, eyes in tapestry,
    Verona chaperons
that fold and deeply twist in painting—
he presides like light caught craftily
on stunning ruby naps, spirit blent
    with cloth next to the flesh.

Thus Venice rises, silken, black-eyed,
with mosaic, alternating heart,
       profoundly dumb. As god
       combs rooms for spoil the mists
of blue night sweep the cool gallery
and stony colonnade. The waters
sough, inch up, and line the palace step
       with finer parallels.

Des Knaben Wunderhorn

How hot it was in Italy.
Whatever bloomed in spring bloomed then
in thorns around your silver head
half hidden in
the vines, the shade.

Your eyes looked out
but something in your hand, hot, flat,
twisted. Birds with their fast hearts
sang further, further, under water,
sped in silence by command.

We were where everything had left
except such disappearances,
save the purple light the arbor
made of dusty trunks in flower.

Field where force had come to rest,
noon a cannon in the blood,
sound the distance to itself
as its old echo died:

You have something in your hand
that touches me, my Lord,
calls me till I wake,
moves along my side.

Heroic Statue in a Garden Run Wild

You exceed the standard by a head,
overtop the goddesses by half,
eloign yourself among the elements
and need no witness and ignore the grass.
The flora of the season overgrows
the granite at your base with peat or rose.

I couldn't reach your elbow at the start.
I sat and felt my head against the greaves.
My rhythms took the beating of your heart,
my melodies the intervals between.
And when I climbed all over you, the rise
of muscle in the calf, bone near the eyes

gave measure to the words you could not speak—
balloons in which the rhomboid, ray, and sine,
the oval, square, triangles on their feet
partitioned out the reaches of your mind—
as though Pythagorean were the beat
of bee and dial, pool and marguerite.

Gabriel

for P. and B.

Blown in from the sidewalk, swept to her stoop,
he always has this look. He takes her in.
The downward ceremonies of her robes
that seem to say she is above occasion
except a languourous incline of the head,
face turning off somewhat, as if, as if—
listening (he thinks, still out of breath) for something
that came from so far, she'd no need to look
for minstrel or the lute, at any rate
no more, now, than the fountain on the stone
or birdsong passing from the underholly
or the muted sprinkle of her hem
on the smooth flags. Desultory and tense,
mysterious her many hours awaiting
who would bring her faith in this address.

Beaming on the threshold in the sun
whose rays crashed after him, he grew august
and logical. He had not known that he
had come to call, but that was what she heard
when, humming on, the rafters fell in place.

Claude Lorrain's "Herdsman," 1655

This is a different sort of heaven.
Man is lying on his back.
Nothing's done that can't as well
be done by things left to themselves.
That Claude is preindustrial
seems odd, for there's the smoke and steam-
mechanic haze at afternoon
upon the glade and river's bed,
the dying branches of the sapling
with some feathered sprays of green,
the brown and browner residue
industry
has painted on the ancient screen.

Environmentalists describe
the Armageddon of the mills
and mines at Bethlehem and Gary
as seductive sylphs of sulfur,
coal, petroleum, and steel
rising from edenic lakes
veiled in scarfs of effluent,
motley as an engine slick—
God's anger spent
on a covenant
whose rainbow fans its stroboscope
above the cities where we breathe.

But air is only dust and dung
in Claude: the *cows* have worn the branches
from their bark (the ground is bright
from their plodding ambulations);
and far off to the right the new
Jerusalem
where granite risers fit the feet
and streets heal over gaps in conversation.

The Tattooer

after the story by Tanizaki

Her toenail and the pearly heel
dissolved by the dark grin of the retreating
palanquin were all he'd seen,
sufficient for his whole career,

Imagination's view of her
complete: the sense of endless thigh
milky as the ponies of the Emperor
above their slender slicing hooves,

his expectation of her skin
a wilderness of intercostal
ice on which her sanguine soul
could be engraved in Ryukyu cinnabar.

Years later—since our fate in these accounts
is after all the fruit of our desires
and sentences in which we crave are those
by which we're doomed—he found her at his door.

Master of a beauty that is pain,
he waited for the ivory girl to wake:
his last and lethal muse with history ahead,
whips in her hair, and from her ribs

to find her breasts, two threads of trembling jet
from the titanic spider he'd emblazoned down her back.

The Pains of Sleep

She throws a gold ax at him.
There is a railing. She jumps it
like a rickety troubadour. Below,
a platform, slick and black.
She sheds her armor for the end.

In the dark above
he beams a bit,
anxious, spousal.

He should have willed her
mottled trout and woodland, all
she could have craved before,
crossing the studded quiver straps
between her ruddy breasts——

He watches, light mouth
filled with fluid, as she sinks.
The coda of the Niebelungs
whines through the mast and nervous
stir of plankton in the wake
as her blood-marbled body falls
through slow-motion witnesses of all her life
and far from the blue pity of his gaze
enters, past the ship's glide.

Elective Affinities

That the night is water
and the day wood
makes it accidental
to be good

Doing what is furthest
Knowing it won't fit
Drawn by nothing human
to your opposite

Pirate to the altar
Ocean to the vault
Kelp torn by the anchor
Goblet drawing salt

Redhead

He wore a tuxedo. We are not liable
for the futile details like evening dress,
but for the terror? Yes.
He had blue gums that something dripped from
and he had known my lock was broken.
He came right in, simply by a whisper from his long
taciturn snout. There are no mammoth in his kind.
He was not tame, he meant me
no kind of good, he was bad but in no wise
anxious or theatrical. He knew
he would kill me slowly
as my eyes could not accustom to the dark
made slightly foul by the dipping
of the broom I know by lore was red
until the thought of his bright teeth and the extreme
narrowness of the face in which they must have lain
would, with the analogous suggestion
of his eyeballs shagged by lazy patience
or the trance of power as he flew
from near to far above the falling
inky floor—would pierce like phosphenes
the wet death of the pillow where my head sank
waiting until the far-off hour
when I knew—we'd been
through this many times—he'd tighten
his circle up to ring my bed,
the bed itself, racing on my body,
baying through my body as the moonlight
began upon my leg and I was, for now, his own.

The Third Casket

Gypsies watched us from behind the man-thick trunks.
Our eyes and face felt white and visible
and surely quick to bleed or to be buried.
Pines the age of earth loomed
wherever we would walk beyond the path
that always ended where we stood. The peaked gable
with a coif of shadowy timber
hiding the eyes seemed to mark our fear.
You slipped the button at my neck and the wind died down.

The cottage window like black water in the hundred
tarns seem from a mountain, into which one sank
down to the middle of the world,
shone at us with the hard negative of a pupil.
Enter, it said.

The bed was piled with fleecy mattresses
no flesh could warm. The icy and familiar keys
of the piano looked about to play, its large cape
of wood risen like a wing.
What was black was infinitely heavy, and exact.
What was white like our fingertips was dead.

Supine and helpless while the worst
weight of our longing, our dark deed,
marched in place through the acres of fir
and the faces that flashed behind them,
my hand fluttered at your smooth cold chest
and the piano with a threatening look
fell rashly through the carbon of the floor.

The Lost World

for George MacDonald 1824–1905

Not those rough magistri of the plot,
engineers of nightmare, Freud and Grimm,
Andersen and Wolfram, that dark lot
painting dramas on the scrim
of all the dreaming world is not
to make us feel more grave within—
who drove to shake the willow tree
fierce horses through our poetry—
      not them again.

Let them ride to where they came,
the Caucasus of passion;
commit ourselves to contemplate
manual and alien
our idle makework at the base
of idea in action.
Deep in the mines the malachite
rises to the moonlight
      in the tow of ocean.

The power that our blindness sought
guys the porous canopy.
Smell of rose and apricot
our lost connection to the sea.
Soap in vases, flame in knots
the shape of buds, the coat of cream—
shadows flutter at the pane,
a painter casting in the rain
      his floating jalousi.

Fishes swim in the flecked air
breathing the rainbow's element.
One color with no name is there.
Shafts rise from the last descent

when we took opal, key, and hair
to seek the old magicians,
familiars then to our desire
but turned now to a babe of fire
       who makes no sense.

When we waken from the dream
day and ordinary brook
rearrange obeying seams,
have a long, transfigured look.
Pools say by our face and feet
how long our adventure took.
But spirits in the turret keep
bowls to plunge us in, to sleep
       by star and rook.

Ovid's Mirror

Had gods existed for a few years more
mythology would not be our sole store

of information on the savage whim
that daggered monarchs and may do us in.

We could consult the rubble at our feet
to monitor the vein where nightmares meet,

read in the summons that we cannot face
the grin of Shuttlecock and Commonplace,

minor deities of vaudeville
who simper and suggest against the kill,

exchange for majesty the double-take
and seltzer water for the burning lake.

You know them. Watch the window where the fly,
the cloth where uninvited fingers, glide

to cross the hostess with her ruined lace
and foul the further trees by carapace.

Or turn toward the contest you have failed
that leaves a horror of tomorrow's mail

made doubly gruesome as it isn't true
we don't half-bank on something coming through.

It's all the work of Caliban and Ptah,
muck, misunderstanding, hem and haw,

with jokes left in the contract that make sense
in no known language, but increase the rent.

It's what myth left behind: despair of friends,
pain when we sleep, the pointed accidents,

nostalgia for a vaguely "native" sin,
suspicion that the outside has no in.

How different from Echo and the Task,
the pool where Longing trembled in his mask—

Ovid's mirror where the curling trees
gave back their faintly girlish jewelry,

where lovers driven down to sunken streams
found how to twin their bodies underneath,

happy endings easy to arrange
if one read the enduring for a change.

And when we stumbled on the Cave of Night
to find there all our hidden, hindered might

still useless baggage, then at least we knew
who to blame, and which Occult was true:

though sex may alter by the dice and urn,
no river tumbles that does not return.

List

Tackle. Paper-clips (bronzette,
serrated). Lift, one-quarter inch,
to raise the left heel of your waders.
Two-faced carpet-tape to make
it stick to sole and to itself.
(Waist now even with the water.)
Tablets of recycled paper
with the answers in the watermark.
That flowered tea that looks like dope.
The small machine that's still on order
which, lowered from the ceiling,
makes frappé and keeps it cold
then fans you to your object in the past
hung like a planet in its cool
and fading rings. (Call about this.)
Batteries. Brochures on game,
birds, flora for the nearsighted
with drawings to scale of the blur
bass form with the current or a nuthatch
makes on the resembling columbine.
Read Hemingway, I. Walton. Take
something to occupy the hands,
something you broke. Consult painters
on the hunt, atlas on
the rivers you may meet,
some blue, some tint with cinnamon.
Prepare a little conversazióne for the hamadryads,
some serviceable front,
Egyptian, tawny, diffident,
but do not turn your back on them. Don't run.
Be tall and of a port in air.
Keep breathing regular. Do not
negotiate when apprehended.
Take what to do while they divine
what you are doing there.

Zeitblom: His Commentary on the Pictures

Her exhibit, we saw, was flawed
but clever. In the Marine Series
where a man in different carapace
and fin embraces the same woman
night after salty, shelving night
there was some guilt, some truth.
Of the Student Subjects, one redhead
(who much resembles a brother of hers)
had charm, a maloccluded jaw,
spots of country color underneath
his open eyes. Students are often
indistinct. He is shown
bearing the phylacteries
in his vague sandy-colored hair.
The early rain and the later rain
counterbalance on the canvas
distinguished by the moments of
their falling. The weak, snuff-umber light
of all these works is bleakly Croat,
lowerclass, no doubt Talmudic.
(Her parents, though, from bourgeois Charleston—
watch for rifts and anguish later on;
an uncle on the mother's side
wrote on the Russian movements of the circus
from Byzantium, ten seventy-three
C. E. Watch for this. Golgotha
she had picked up on her own.)
Dream panels for the reredos
which she told some of us, aside,
would be called "The Endless Mutiny,"
commissioned by that crippled priest
for the Zwingli Mission in, I think,
Raron (where Rilke, no?) depend
in story-broken strips. In one

(in several) she is seated, a navy
bow of watered taffeta
always at her right temple, perhaps
for frontlets, for a sign. Young men
stand and press against her puzzled
form. The theme's desire in *them*
carried out in inner mutinies,
in the oak-gold eye, the bowl in her hand,
the chasteness of the bodice cloth
where Tudor thorn and panicle
weave and confuse. Her mouth is beautiful,
shocking, quite unlike the painter's:
she is the old Love figure.
Yearning in others. Pressure. Dreams
that make what may be unbearably tender
and false. Dreams that are power-ridden.
Rilke, the Sonnets, Wera who died
at nineteen. It's all irrefutably there.

"He Was Everywhere He Had Ever Been"

—William Hunt, *Oceans and
Corridors of Orpheus* (1979)

How fine to say that of oneself
and not despair. To find
curls in the fretted locket
that belong to one
who sleeps beside you, woven
in your dream; how fine to see
gazing from the still water
the various slides of yourself
aged three, tasting salt;
aged ten when you learned
"veranda"; at twenty in a Burne-Jones
corridor, you're that redhead
with combs in her mane
figuring on a sudden
savior come down from the marble loft;
until the present mirror of routine
visitations has you facing each other,
twin regents struck for a coin.

But to that clear commerce throng
terrors in hieroglyph. At three the pool
shows how the black water climbed
to my bib. The pool of all near-truth
says I died at ten to the world
where language applies because I
had found I was wicked and never learned.
The worsening of expectation
continues, through loud but trivial

shocks in the twenties
as the answers dropped coolly down
to my pallet
             where now, at a certain age
unwilling to die, I am falling
into myself, into so many
strange insignia petrified
by the same fire.

Period Pieces

in memory of Earl R. Wasserman

(Note: While I do not pretend that these "period pieces" are necessarily just to their models, I hope that the principle of imitation, in the poems that follow, in some small way resembles the discipline of Earl Wasserman's attention to the eighteenth- and nineteenth-century texts he wrote about and taught. I have never seen anyone who kept the text in front of him so constantly, who returned to it so loyally. His thought was not original, but practically unique in another way: he was not trying to devise interpretations for the poetry, but rather to school himself to think like his subjects. There was thus always something uncanny behind the energy of Professor Wasserman's scholarship, something like ventriloquism in his arguments, as if he were attempting to do for Shelley and Wordsworth, Keats and Pope, what Pierre Menard wanted to do for Cervantes—reincarnate a lost sensibility word for word.)

I. Drydenian Couplets

Hurt comes upon us as (in broken time,
to rhyme while seeming to excuse the rhyme,

refusing to admit the worst we know
yet idly do the thing we most do show)

something unspecified—as marching tunes
on vacant afternoons

occur to us without their melodies
or as a secret game among the Pleiades

taught from a height where we can't hear the words,
in throws we cannot catch, rules too absurd.

We know their purpose but without the meaning,
though that's understood, or, gazing, leaning,

pacing to the metres of the wood,
our forehead to the grain, we feel we could.

But after motion, quiet, madness in the pot;
the cutlery recalls what we forgot.

Insults run in columns, absent lives
fill up like dirty drawers with butcher knives.

Endearments that end nowhere still comprise
the dim half-language of the suicide,

syntactify the sound we only moan
or drive us semi-conscious to the phone.

Had Love come radiant in sentences,
had Seraphs answered at the other end

to tell the words we utter in distress
the way to get from words to wordlessness,

we would not have to haggle with the years
or turn again to eat our bread with tears.

II. *After Three Consecutive Nights of Dreaming About Alexander Pope*

Crookbacked—I must have read he was—and reined
   by cloudy telepathic lines to several brace
   of tiny silken dogs with Algarotti's face,
      Pope stands upon the chamber's cold parquet
and tells the swaying figure of the queen,
      "Your love is pox'd, and libelous your hate."

Lady Mary moves, exalted by her shame,
   his censure worthy in that it was vile,
to the grotto's pulsing spring, alike the gauge
   by which to time her heartbeats and this smile:
"Correct, dear Pope, for in our bloody age
   the dreams of mangled poetry are right."

Neither one, though fine, was made for art,
   his spine a lover's knot and pocked her skin.
      Pope's evil sycophants and eccentricity,
   hers that she was mistaken in her men.
      "The best of passions, Love and Fame," wrote Eloise,
whose author's armor far outshone his heart.

Yet in the final stanza of the dream
　　the figures stay, the candelabrum flickering
　　　　on bits of tin and bottle stuck in clay
　　whence the river of resemblance from that century
that runs in brown along the curb of sleep
　　　　keeps A and M, crossed complements, at bay

like souls so light and dry upon the shore
　　who wait for their translation into life,
the very breeze about the landing boat
　　blows them back the moment it arrives:
the words of human comfort in the throat
　　are turned by their strange diction into lies.

III. *Indiana Limestone*

As if the sun had started weakening
when it approached the porches of the day,
it did not grow to bronze, it was not gay.
The tulip stood. A wind of kerosene

blew just like air. The sunbeam's aureole
colorless as a communion wafer
fell loudly gray upon the Sunday paper,
the rituals turned editorial.

Automatic sounds the call to waken
broadcast from an automatic score.
The carillon of noon rings redder, colder.

I look into the eye of my beholder
in whom the sky and tulip are restored
and read a verdict on the road not taken.

It was not we who changed, it was the odd
formation of the place, Ravel, bouquets,
sofas passion long ago had frayed.
Strange, that we should but now have thought of God

as if the look of paisley in defeat
were one way to get through the world to Him.
In Jesus' name we tore us limb from limb
while belfries tolled accounts in clanging feet

and program music to the beaten boulevards
that, like the streets in Zola, slowly drifted
away from anything to touch—which lifted

nothing from the shoulders of the poor
and put the parallels right to our door
and smelled of oil of orange in the dark.

IV. *The Nordic Twilight*

Green the close sky,
gun-metal the wave.
Black chevrons with eyes
where we would grieve
swoop to that place.

Cry of the predator,
scream of the self.
Traffic in semaphore
guides a diaspora
gathered to death.

Face at the window,
toy under steel.
Crippled the hoe,
crippled the heel:
old commonweal

of workers, the dying,
gardeners, hangmen,
starting from sleeping,
keeping from crying,
succeeding ill.

Children pull sleds
up the inhuman ice,
thorns in their eyes.
Where the heart lies,
stone instead.

Where we waken,
dwarf evergreens
looking like men,
berries' blue shine
looking like eyes.

Dawn brought the maidens
holding their breath,
doling out endings
that they had left,
white and malign.

Watch from the roof,
watch from the stair.
Mirrors are proof
one passes there
into the future

whither it stole
telling the forest
from its black body
tales of iron,
turrets of coal.

V. Saving the Romantics

If we found wisdom beyond term
in measures that stopped cold, a human
token of conclusion in
a shapèd end, whatever called,
like twilight outline and command,

then loose ends launched our feeling for
the words and certainties adrift
just as Adam had to choose between
sleep, ripe plums, a noontide merging
with divinely seeded earth,
and tasks that waited to be given names.

The poem was this patience, a preserve
or place for feeling what preparedness
suddenly enabled, and practice,
and the inseam of an awkward
pose, willingly prolonged—
the coil from nothingness, discomfort,
into desperate accident,
swift, apostate, but achieved.

Even in their themes they stood between
care for the old (the plain and magical,
the phrenological twist, the doom
of human love, waterfall
and thorn), and the search on our behalf
for new anxiety (the haunted wrest
of soul from bone by virtue of idea).
Perhaps I eat, wrote Keats, that I persuade
myself I am, and many times, on Wordsworth's
way to school, he'd pull at walls and trees
to save himself from falling into an empty field,
clinging with his might to a stile, or post,
that he not be whirled into what wasn't him.

These were the first Romantics
as they labored to arrive:
vessels and seeded earth, merely.
A path God walked at dusk without a sign.
A place of few markers but,
to real sun through mist, and choking fog,
a breathing earth from which self-spanning strained.

Scenes from the Liturgy

> He sings to me
> behind blue windows.
> He sings to me
> as jewelled bells.
>
> —Marina Tsvetayeva

Low-lying masses of fog have disappeared
and, though you are lost, a corner has been turned.
There at the crossing, standing ready
and bereft of every leaf, the limbs of trees,
black sharpened styluses, begin
to carve their puzzling paralyzed
commandments on the blue beyond.

The ground has frozen. Yellow ice forms on
the inside of the windows like a caul.
At the corner of the pane, a Jew in red.
Ornaments from Belgrade, Sweden, Krakow, and Korea
twist from drying boughs in the smoky light.
Human figures do not move between the airs,
here are only words or painted things
though no thing moves: the smell of juniper
remembered with its sour blue berries
hidden in the thick and gray-tinged green,
a sallow rouge upon the silent cloth,
gilding on the angel's leaden wing,
enciphered glass in vague but secret
scrolls—the turning of a brook, light through the lids,
the face of memory in a ragged hat
or on its skates, the icy glare of minor gods
and minor drunkenness. "Manager"
keeps coming out for "manger," where He lay.
Strange, isn't it? this worship of a babe?
Oaks caused the same derangement in the Tribes,
the seeing of what isn't there, but is to be.

The silence rises like a choir
of Aged Ones who swim the vacant air,
blue corded arm to watery thigh,
beholding from their shining heads with conscious eyes.
Some ribbons move. An angel sighs and guides
his back to you as, ruby, lime,
the vitreous splendors of the bells
toll forth upon this remnant godless place
their cozening remorse.

It is not always possible to pray.
I would to God have rain for all the places
where winds lash on and spread the fires,
limberness for dancers, light in the muffled sky;
sarabands by gifted spirits
with conceding hearts—may they
transform the air to music,
real and hardly human. As for the endless
fallings in the night, grant that when
the shining sands, the ones we call our mirrors,
beckon from the darkness of
the parlor or the bath,
we find the pools from which, *en face,*
forgiven life looks up.

I had planned to read that wall of books,
pinning each idea to its pattern.
But few techniques have broken on me,
and a few ideas, as beautiful.
Is that it?
      Iseult of Brittany
moving her white hands on the bandage?
Someone looking wistfully to sea
while sinking occurs? Final losses
that do not register in the heart
any longer, since pain was constant
at the end throughout?
           Some things to do
with prepositions, thorn gone into
the head, grace come in at the eye, for
and without, by and through and toward,
are all I have learned from history.

Acting

on Ariane Mnouchkine's *Molière*

Grief at his death let it through.
They ran with him up the stairs
the film said, and the film said
he was bleeding from his throat
as through a dark passageway
from the pale, weary waters
that had fountained their living
and done with their bottom land.
There, said blood.
                    God please let me
breathe.
            From the groundfloor riser
to the fourth or seventh step
took several heated hours.
Sweat broke on their collarbones
and wept away their coiffeurs,
tangled the cords forever
on capes that clapped in dismay,
flying from their necks like hope.
Don't let this be, they whispered.

Elsewhere a thin gondola
black with a gold dragon prow
was being pulled to Versailles.
The waters rose from the past,
shifted massive in their sleep,
dimpling as their surfaces
stretched under the first dewfall.
He'd been cold since the first act
of the play—and now the torches,
his mother in their rocking,

in their fever, danger, sleep
but for this jostling din.
His old friends held him by knee
by arm by bloody placket,
weeping as they pulled him on.

O God let me let me breathe.

As with players it was hard
to know which part was drama
in the paralyzed ascent,
which, their more visible love,
they dug their evening slippers
into each hard step
and ran with him to the end.

Negatives

for William Hunt

Here on the mantel by your lifted head,
playing its white hands toward your smile
and pointing to the dinner hour (the sped
inviting blackness of the summer light
straying from the frame's determined sights),
the mechanism of the snapshot clock,
crystal, cog, and gravamen, is caught

in the helpless working negative
that serves as memory in aftertime
when time conceals the beat by which it lived,
its documentary the blurring line
within the works—a dynamo, but quiet,
whose dark wheel shows white, our blood
the only proof of life on the pale drum.

In that backwards room where nothing ever
happened, where the deadly turbines lived
against whom we grew feeble, you turned your clever
temporary head, full of ideas,
toward the somber relatives—
but what were you thinking? what were you about
to say to someone when the light went out?

     *   *   *

That is the background; it is far from clear.
Light-and-dark the dialect of mind
in eye, which cannot compensate the ear
that listens for the patterning of time—
cannot clarify the lighting of the light
by which, the guest departing down the stair,
I lay my loving wrists into his hair.

Is it not strange? A moment earlier,
semblance, parable, the sunny chair,
attempts to ration truth as a demurral.
Then suddenly my eyes upon the air
could find no instrument, no blade to pare
the what I thought of once as being there
from what I saw transfigured as the here.

It is like love I thought, I thought, I thought.
Leaves lay folded brown into the tree,
waving with the branches (as they ought),
yet messengers, the governors, the freed.
Trouble was of old. You came to me,
minister to loneliness and lack,
the countenance I always wanted back.

Even as it's thought, that is not true:
polarity between one and another
does not persist beyond the moment you
unpack your case, cross out the hard word *lover,*
welcome back the habits rage had smothered—
how they emerge like turrets from the mist,
the even lines of bedding, thorn, and wrist.

     *   *   *

When we have returned from the emotions
where we had urged the fair to stay a while,
the bald gaze of the bench at our devotions
and of the sink, the doormat's ravelled edge,
the tub, the stair, comprise a peristyle
within whose temple close our mystery
lets down its awful taproot like a tree,

touching at the outset what is cold,
metal bars, precisely soldered bronze,
leftover treasure, under-offered bowls,
then something briefly warm, the willow wands
of myth, shell of the sea, a leaf of celadon.
The eerie moon glows large within the grove,
escaped from darkness like a human love.

Mirror on the wall, face in our sleep,
rain-displacing pulse, the body grown,
these are the quantities we keep,
the company of seedling to the sown,
evasion by the knower of the known.
Places are within us like the stream
that carries us from power into dream.

*   *   *

The dream was nothing much, was everything.
Trifles work profoundly, in reverse.
With these ambassadors of comforting,
bearded men, and sensual, and terse,
I always want the Good and act the Worse.
Symbolically, they do not have to speak
(but do). The foyer talks in filagree.

Although setting should not matter, in the dream
the place and color are so severed
from the glancing run of life, they *mean*.
Copses, at the turning of a lever,
fan their wordless undersides of silver.
Fingers brush our eyes in amity.
Electric cords converge in polities

for government by insignificance.
The fallen star sleeps lightly in the reeds.
Even lumber-jackets are complex.
Tissues of the body pulse like seas.
The gesture of the other lightens me
and meaning, meaning, meaning, like the blues
pours from the chosen as they cannot choose.

What's wanted shall be given, what we voice
in arbitrary versions is made clear.
A bird looks at us with the landscape's choice
of us as reservoirs of what is dear—
when were we ever pivotal as here?
(Have we only made this joy from pieces
the reasonable life will take to pieces?)

   *   *   *

The waking heart still leaps up to the light,
a sailing bird imprisoned by the wind
that drags its feathers' hachure from the right,
torn to a halt except the branches bend.
We ask: what is it, coming to an end?
We ask aloud the world that waits on us.
The world can only answer as it must.

And did it say (we think we heard this said),
"Have you believed that dream about two Bays,
the Good and Bad Bay, curled on either side
of an island risen from dark humid leaves?
We put a question in the leaves,"
it answered in the asking,
"We mean the azure imagery
for meanings you can't see."

Was it true
one must not take that blue—oh more than sky
held to the lasting quivering still light,
more than the blue on milky coves, black springs, alluvial
tideflats scalloped by the hunter's boot—
take them for anything? Or the oily rime,
Bad Bay's fluid peril, for benign?

" 'You will yet marry me,' " I say, "he said.
'Come. Love. Relinquish. Disappearing, be.' "
He had a green gaze in his bearded head
and that meant, "Will you follow me?"
and that meant, "Here is probity."
His hands with their rough nails meant storm,
his rumpled collar meant the calm.

But someone's right: we drown in that we wake
as though the thin and ordinary air
were thicker than the red satanic lake
or than the marriageable stare
of men who flood our hearts until we wake—
as though the brilliant dream ran through a stubborn sieve,
the dawn bled out and final like the figure in a negative.

To Gustavus Adolphus in Basic Training

Where in the whole night air
are you, with a haversack,
damp boots, perhaps a flare?
Are you tonight on exercise
on foot, tilting the compass
up to the night's anxious glow?

I live on a street of practice
bells, civilian false alarms,
the blacks who've served. I fear the theft
in a three-quarters furnished room
of something other than a chair,
something wry, and quietly concealed.

Where in the broad oat plain
do you have lunch—in a landscaped
shrub? atop a spur? Do you
have to rub your face against
your hand when the tawny wind
rakes across your chest, your pack?

I need, it seems, to question you,
to ask you how you read these racks
of coded sunlight from the shades,
to ask you to decipher—you:
how you'd look to me when I
can't see, how you'd think of gestures

you don't note, how you'd really
see yourself as I could see you
(not knowing yet what I think of all this
since you refuse). It is the mutual
devotion, that I miss, of circumstance
to method, of the method to the purposive.

I counted ten on the underside
of your arm; in portrait, spreading
plums above your ribs. The next time
I expect ten fresher purple
marks beside your knees, from grasping
fictive ropes, in fierce conditions.

Reading During Marriage

Comic the drawl of small rain
down the wavering windows
poorly fitted to their sills.
Winter sees us reconciled,
lamp lights absurdly golden
pouring their slow pools across
nap, binding, and fluted shade.
We each have a book to read
and laugh at the odd moment.

All countries are implied here
in the dusk between covers,
Russia at night and Ireland
by moonlight—Dostoievski,
Bowen. Roubles the color
of the rainbow will obtain,
in Cork up in the hot eaves
of the stone manor, the dress
ancestral that your double
wore. Brought to it by instinct,
iridescent, powerful
mirror gratuitously
reflecting what you can want
against the longing it cost,
you smile into your shadow.
Women. Best writers, best wives,
devisers of that twilight
toward which all things tend.

Mortally tired but nothing
wasted I see the fair sweep
(as you depart the carriage
wheel scoring her muff with snow)
of my face in your regard:

this no older than I am,
that no longer discouraged.

Asked to Recall
a Moment of Pure Happiness

The bed's height is one reason
for floating. It is near noon.
Again you have overslept.

On the Hotel Belvedere
a triangle of sunlight
bites across the reddish bricks,
but in the alley's camera
the bulk are in blue shadow
that glints off the iron grille
of your fire stairs, or cages.
This happy imprisonment
makes no sense, yet is not false.
Your life is starting over.

Traffic moans from the other
room that floods with yellow day.
The little hallway of shelves
between that dazzling ceiling
and this murkier, blue one
fills with a loose corolla,
ambiguous and humming.

Life, day, shadowy iron
and sun, whispering taxis,
heat at the end of summer
raising a mist on your skin,
Eager Street, Charles, Mt. Vernon,
Biddle, St Paul—in their arms
you float into your future.

Stone Lake

Brown water, bright sand.
Black minnows dart through
like the brushstrokes you
have made with your hand
in a shifting dream,

forgetful as seams
raised by the slow, warm
wind before a storm,
broken by sunbeams
casting down pattern.

Wading, you may learn
how the wave rises
in language that says
cool and warm by turns
as fish brush by you.

Where the Storm Goes

The goal of its migration is where you are standing
as the long hour rumbles in. The storm is being
pulled into the orbit of your post, heading straight for you
as the various small life run to your leaning porch with its
long low shoebox of rainless air. They cluck
their passionless remarks on the screen
and then go still, the birds have all gone still, spiders
sweep the damp cement of the portico like ebbing hair
as though somebody had already drowned, yet they are aimless
                and there's
no drama in their routes, no shape appealed to.

It may be that the foothills of some range go blank
and distance disappears or slaps toward you
as the lightning wonders for held moments over the faun-soft
gray of the trunks of youthful trees and the first
woodnotes of the almost instant thunder admonish you.
That was exciting in its way but did not seem like the hard point
                of the storm.
Rather pale, in fact, so perhaps the real center was the next gush
                of the
rain, white as milk, solid as a mountain—the communicating
tissue between the fall line and yourself that you could walk
                through
like a looking-glass into the distance where all things reverse and
                touch.

Yet the middle vortex, the most secret center of the storm,
falls to the world and keeps on looking for you.

Bound Man

By day the dial tells the wrong time
with its fiercely anchored blade.
Stars by night in toughened shapes
swing flat across the passing sky.
Reality is something light falls through
or dies against, that so solid, this so briefly blue.

Ghost at Dawn

Presence—when the street hauls its coil
out to the heavy corners of the town,
when the dull lead grains of light build their swarms
in the former absolute of the blackened room
like something growing in the air and the stair
hums with meaning, which the myrtle bush repeats
and which, from its far stream, the wheel of soaring
yet distinctly calling birds seems to direct—
you are here.
                    Summer in the yard,
close, clinging, beckons through the window
to this old man, my grandfather, already
organizing on the floor below
the way my wakening, and the morning light,
would form itself from air, and go from there.

                *   *   *

My father left on a trip, or we all left
(sometimes these journeys hard to tell apart),
the hour of the wolf the hour of departures—
fearful, since each shape was slow, and live.
Pajama pattern, chair, slat on the stair
seemed to contract, breathe, move an inch to one side.
In the yard the rough trunk of an apple tree,
due to this rearranging, breathing light,
frayed out to a wedge of them facing us
around the shoulder of the tree before.

I was in bed when I knew I was awake
and that the house was under observation.
There was the sound of breathing from the others,

from my sister beside me, coherent in stillness.
No exaggeration of dish, no light, and no heat.
When I got downstairs my brother was at the window.
You could barely tell it was snowing because of the gray
shimmer of molecules, as the roofs of the place
hardened to get back where they were before him.
My brother shivered. *We are moving,* he said.
But he was asleep. My father would come to get us.

*   *   *

My lover was in the Marines, even then a dying
calling in compact for harm. Discipline,
still stiff about the seed of comradeship,
drew from him that hoarse dusty loyalty
like helpless love-of-family in the heart
that beat beneath the hard white plate of muscle
readiness and work had formed him to—
beating in its strong subversive way
like the hope he had, to alter from within
the steel protocols of harm that had no point
by suggesting the red vessels (which they lacked)
whose tribute could be circular, yet true.

For many months before they made it inhuman
for him to live with his life in their arms,
they made his task severe; casual
in the way of power to spare; sinister
as only that can be which strikes one way
and disappears another, until the night
collected all its forces late one night
into a flat Potomac dawn, making
clear the sentence that he wasn't there,
that day without him couldn't help but hurt.

*   *   *

For the past two mornings I have been up at five,
awakened by something I couldn't identify.
Yesterday, this was so: I stood by the window
looking out at myself and trying to go back to sleep.
There was something in the corner, a heap of dark
that hadn't made it yet into its place.
This morning, it was so: but now I knew
what the peppery sidewalk and pale slime of the roofs
were meant to say.

           In the dream a baby,
blond, and talking directly from his birth,
had been taken away from me. To the nurses
and a sparse clutch of relatives I added,
You see, to all my remarks and could not weep,
feeling the cold where his curve had lapped my front.
News got out. Someone was called in.

I believe I was typing in the hospital,
unable to move my neck in my distress,
when a large fat figure in an overcoat
brought in a large fat bundle of light: *my child.*
I did not know, as I unwrapped the blanket,
that children grew so much from day to day.
Suddenly fearful, I wondered if he knew me,
but in the limitless of his attention
I was answered: he spoke plain to my questions,
stroked my hair (he loved me best of all),
and then he breathed, moving in my fingers
like a scarf, taut, iridescent, real,
and (this the message weaving in the cirrus
of his gaze)
           he was not anywhere.

Looking Back

You would not speak of what was not right here.
What grieved me when I died was that
dying was the note you could not hear.
You would not speak. Of what was not, right here
(singing on the threshold of the year)
or in the night that came, to come—that
you would not speak of. What was not right here,
what grieved me when I died, was that.

Old People's Holiday

Now that we are all dead, no matter.
Snow recedes from the trees,
hulls of hemisphere where the trunks go in,
and we've come back to the den where we spent our
children's lives playing games that were extinct
in foreign languages we'd forgotten how to speak.

Furniture we preferred as it was dated
lines the walls. Down the hall
on nails hang unimportant papers
poorly framed. And in the den
perfused with the aroma of a recipe
for which the commonest ingredients
could not in this country be obtained
(where could you find the salty knob
of chalk from the sea?), once shiny
pens in consoles that don't work,
peeling poker chips, desk and lamp
in laminates of cherry, calf, and jade.
We thought they were so pretty.
We still do.

Who would have thought there were so many
shades of imitation
or that we slept the more secure
to own them? that the men who made them
(canasta stands from marl, divans from shale)
would have seen, beneath the presses,
iron-hearted plastic forming
by the bosses' template into rich
dark woods, the birdseye-maple ribbons
of the free and earned and artificial day?

When you hold them to the light
the hard nubs of your fingers still shine through.

Coming On Again

You shouldn't feel this way when you are sick.
Riddling with nausea the least thread of desire,
illness calls forth other appetites
as for the short rope into nothing,
careful, white, but not
too vivid and no bass beating in the pool
of the temples: however cool the stave
your head can't take it, however sweet
that swimmer in the dark weeds of your dream,
you don't want to be touched at such low fathom.

Note how you come up as from a dive
the eighth day of your wet white voyage
on the bed, behind your eyes the drab
drumbeat that won't die out, the gullies
where you've lain, the grainy muslin
and loose surf of objects on the table
next to the clock that harshly kept on counting. . . .
Yet you move a part of you and nothing roars.
A knee won't tip your head into the tunnel.
To your surprise your arm won't pierce your eyes.
The ice has melted in the mattress ticking
and the ghastly furnace in the bedspread's out.
Can you see your way clear?

                          Try to read
labels or the butterfly of pages
and English grows the most illusive letters,
fat, shadowy, and porous and its prose
comes off oily on your thumb or poetry
dazzles with its commas in the white.
Both pain and explanation make you sick
and you're less free than ever. Recuperating
in this threatened backditch of the field,
tentflaps barely fluttering, air foul,
light uncertain, where you are in doubt,

here it comes through the awful fog,
what you felt coming on again.

You know you're nearly well when you stand up,
put on a belt successfully, and feel
the old blade twisting in the solar plexus.
Your foot cramps over the same scruple in your shoe
and your eyes, that feel so raw and don't know where to turn,
do as they do because the scales have fallen from them
and fall even as you look on all the old resolves.

Novum Organum

Mother of disturbance
Madam of each sigh
Pander to significance
Patron of the shy

Crutches of the feeble
Text of all disease
Daemon of placebo
Rotten mask of need

Lioness of torture
Furnace of the true
Wheel that cures by breaking
you of what you do

The Quest

for Mary Etta Knapp

Like an old duchessa who has talked all night
whom the Republic's leaders have forgotten,
Venus is guided up the dim cone of rooms,
still glowing through her empty outpost
alone among already vanished stars.

The sun increases in her wake.
Putting off his moony Dutch enamel
for direct Baroque, the young retainer
hales up in repeated ormolu
a cold, new wind in the clicking trees.

At the corner of the garden
as that surprised vague rash
on a nearly white Bosc
grows into smiling russet
from far enough away,
an adolescent beech
thrusts his pride of bristling opal
from the matted lawn,
blushing when you look back
from the verge.

But among that litter of leaf as the gate closes
you have seen, between the bony poplars there, and there,
a few bright charms tied in yellow to the twigs
to tell you in the blowing forest where you should have turned.